WRITERS AND THEIR WORK: NO 208

Angus Wilson

by K. W. GRANSDEN

Published for the British Council
and the National Book League
by Longmans, Green & Co

Three shillings and sixpence net

Angus Wilson, one of the most highly esteemed of contemporary English novelists, has now been publishing for twenty years: his first collection of short stories, *The Wrong Set*, appeared in 1949. Most of his work deals with English character; 'he records with great accuracy the changing idiom, habits and other fashions of English society in his lifetime,' writes Mr Gransden and notes that, apart from its other qualities, Wilson's work is valuable as social documentary.

Angus Wilson was born in England and spent most of his childhood in hotels in the south of England and at a London public school. His mother was South African and he visited that country for the first time when he was nine. After leaving Oxford, he joined the staff of the British Museum, and his work there gave him an understanding of the 'cultural Establishment' which forms the subject of several stories and novels, including *The Old Men at the Zoo* and the play *The Mulberry Bush*. Another central theme is the decline of liberal-humanism and the plight of intellectuals in post-war Britain. Wilson is both the heir and the satirical critic of the tradition represented by the 'Bloomsbury Group', the coterie which included the economist Lord Keynes, the novelists Virginia Woolf and E. M. Forster and the biographer, Lytton Strachey. In his first two novels, *Hemlock and After* and *Anglo-Saxon Attitudes*, Wilson reveals the weakness of this tradition as well as its strength, and relates this world of high culture and spiritual values to very different *milieux*. Besides his novels and short stories, Wilson has also published much literary journalism and criticism, and has given talks on both the radio and television.

K. W. Gransden is a Lecturer in English at the University of Warwick. After graduating at Cambridge he was for some years an Assistant Keeper in the Department of Manuscripts at the British Museum. His publications include: *Any Day* (poems), a study of E. M. Forster (in the 'Writers and Critics' series), and an essay on Tennyson's *In Memoriam*. He is at present working on Elizabethan satire.

Acknowledgments: Thanks are due to the publishers, Martin Secker and Warburg Ltd, for permission to include extracts from the works of Angus Wilson. The frontispiece photograph is by Tony Garrett.

ANGUS WILSON
by
K. W. Gransden

Edited by Ian Scott-Kilvert

CENTRAL MISSOURI
STATE COLLEGE
Warrensburg

ANGUS WILSON

ANGUS WILSON

by

K. W. GRANSDEN

PUBLISHED FOR
THE BRITISH COUNCIL
AND THE NATIONAL BOOK LEAGUE
BY LONGMANS, GREEN & CO

LONGMANS, GREEN & CO LTD,
Longman House, Burnt Mill, Harlow, Essex

*Associated companies, branches and
representatives throughout the world*

First published 1969
© K. W. Gransden, 1969

*Printed in Great Britain by
F. Mildner & Sons, London, EC1*

ANGUS WILSON

I

A NGUS WILSON has himself provided some fascinating information about his life in relation to his early fiction in *The Wild Garden, or Speaking of Writing*, originally a series of lectures given in California in 1960 and first published in 1963, fourteen years after the appearance of his first book of stories, *The Wrong Set* (1949). *The Wild Garden* also corrects a misconception—the South African childhood referred to in the Penguin editions of his books. Though his mother was South African, Wilson did not visit that country till he was nine; his childhood was largely passed in hotels in the South of England and at a London public school. Only one of his early stories, 'Union Reunion', has a South African setting.

Childhood and the family forms the deepest autobiographical layer in Wilson's fiction. It is also perhaps the most English of all literary subjects: Wilson writes here in the tradition of E. M. Forster and Christopher Isherwood. The mother in his devastating attack on 'the family', 'Mother's Sense of Fun', is akin to Mrs Lindsay in Isherwood's *All the Conspirators*. A disgusted view of family life is seen in the story 'Union Reunion'. The lonely sensitive child is the subject of the story 'Necessity's Child' (in the second book of stories, *Such Darling Dodos* 1950). Rodney, neglected by his smart-shallow parents, escapes into fantasy like the boy in Forster's story 'The Celestial Omnibus', though the form taken by the fantasy is significantly different. The hearty clergyman in Wilson's story resembles Mr Bons in 'The Celestial Omnibus' and Mr Pembroke in Forster's novel of sensitive childhood, *The Longest Journey*. Wilson's Rodney tries to make himself interesting to adults by romancing: first he pretends that his mother is ill, then

5

that a kindly old couple he met on the 'front' (the story is set in an English seaside town) have shown him obscene pictures. In his final fantasy he imagines his parents are drowned, with confused memories drawn from his reading —the sinking of the *Titanic* in 1912 and of the *Pequod* in *Moby Dick*. A more violent version of this fantasy occurs in 'Mummy to the Rescue', while another story, 'Mother's Sense of Fun', also ends with a nightmare in which Donald (whose mother, like Rickie's in *The Longest Journey*, has really died) realizes that 'she had tied him to her and now she had left him for ever'.

But whereas in Forster's 'Celestial Omnibus' the boy's fantasy about the bus that goes to heaven is 'truer' and more beautiful than the prosaic 'reality' of the adult world, in 'Necessity's Child' this idealistic resolution is characteristically rejected. Forster's concept of salvation through innocence becomes in Wilson a matter of makeshift, of 'getting by' in the corrupt adult world by using its own language of disgust. The irony of the story lies in the fact that the timid Rodney gains through his lies a false reputation for being 'a very brave boy'. The pressures of adult selfishness on the child's mind produce in him the sort of revenge-fantasy from memories of which, years later, Wilson himself was to start writing. In his earliest story, 'Raspberry Jam', the obscene reminiscence of two crazy drunken old women 'was largely meaningless to the boy, though he remembered it in later years'.

Wilson wrote 'Raspberry Jam', probably the most horrific of his stories, in 1946, when he was thirty-three, at a time of personal crisis and conflict. He was then an Assistant Keeper in the Department of Printed Books at the British Museum, from which he resigned in 1955 to become a full-time writer. Several of his early stories can be seen as attempts to come to terms with the past, in order to shape the future into something new. This pattern in his own life is reflected in the lives of the central characters of several of his novels, e.g. Gerald Middleton in *Anglo-Saxon Attitudes*.

II

The Museum is both a great centre of scholarship and a department of the Civil Service, and is unofficially linked in a nexus of influence to the world of the universities, the art galleries and the BBC. Wilson's work there gave him an understanding of the management of English high culture, which forms the second important 'layer' in his work. He used his experience of this world in several stories, in the first two novels, and later in *The Old Men at the Zoo*, where the Zoo stands in a kind of transposition for the Museum (or any other great institution) and the 'old men' are the traditional administrators who belong to the Athenaeum Club, cover up their errors and conceal their private inadequacies behind the 'image' of the system.

The Museum also stands in Bloomsbury, the quarter of London associated earlier in this century with an influential intellectual coterie which included E. M. Forster, Leonard and Virginia Woolf, Lord Keynes and Lytton Strachey. Of this liberal-humanist tradition Wilson is both the spiritual heir and the satirical critic.

The cultural 'Establishment' is also the milieu of Wilson's only stage-play, *The Mulberry Bush* (1956), which deals with one of his central themes: the dilemma of intellectual idealists in post-1945 England. The play opens with the retirement from a college headship of Professor Padley, a high-minded member of a famous liberal family. He says of his successor, a new-style bureaucrat (the situation resembles that in an earlier story, 'Realpolitik'): 'I've no doubt that his great business acumen will be of inestimable service to the college in these days of high-powered administration.' The irony here is not just against the bureaucrat, unlikeable though he is clearly meant to be: it is also against Padley himself, who uses the hallowed language of reasonableness yet cannot emotionally face the fact that society has rejected his ideals and values. The decline of the liberal tradition forms the theme of the first two novels and also of the story 'Such Darling Dodos', in which opposition to the Oxford radical-humanism of Robin and Priscilla (the Dodos of the title) comes from an ironically-handled, intellectually meaningless alliance between the younger generation (for whom the nineteen-thirties is almost a dirty word for the failure to make ideals work) and Cousin Tony, an elderly Catholic aesthete: when Tony is told by the students that his cousins are living in the past 'he hadn't felt so modern since the first production of L'Après-Midi'.[1]

Most of Wilson's middle-aged liberals are nagged by feelings of self-doubt, failure or guilt, yet they continue emotionally to accept the Victorian ideals of progress and enlightenment in which they were brought up. The phrase 'all the things there are to do' in The Mulberry Bush is almost an echo of Tennyson's 'so much to do, so little done'.

The weakness of liberal humanism in post-1945 England is demonstrated in much of Wilson's work by weakness on the part of its adherents in the one field they traditionally most respected—that of personal relations. They fail because they cannot practise what they preach. Some of them are so obsessed with scruples about their own motives that they cannot act at all; they are moral paralytics. In The Wild Garden Wilson speaks of the 'tragic paradox' that 'the self-knowledge necessary to bridge the chasm' between liberal intentions in personal relations and actual failure becomes 'itself the agent of the stultified will'.

The most positive character in The Mulberry Bush is Professor Padley's protégé Peter, who gives up historical research (which equals 'truth') for administration ('power') rather than accompany the Professor on yet another 'do-gooding' mission. (The play is contemporary with the novel Anglo-Saxon Attitudes which also explores the relationship between historical research and 'getting things done'.)

[1] A famous land-mark in twentieth-century art—the production by Diaghilev of the ballet L'Après-Midi d'un Faune (music by Debussy) in Paris, 1912.

Peter is accused of abandoning ideals, but for him his choice represents the saving of all the Padleys stood for, without all the patronage and self-satisfaction, the helping hand extended so readily to criminals and misfits. This charge of self-indulgence is also brought by implication against Bernard in *Hemlock and After*. Similarly, in *Anglo-Saxon Attitudes* Mrs Middleton's left-wing idealism is shown up as the sentimental stupidity of a rich woman when she takes into her house a charming Irish boy who is in fact a homosexual layabout and a thief, who later nearly destroys her son John. (One thinks here also of Ernest's attempts to reform prostitutes in Butler's *The Way of All Flesh*.)

In *The Mulberry Bush* Peter says 'Just because the Padleys have gone dead, it doesn't mean it can't be done: it can, but not here, not in their way. I have the sense to face reality.' This—facing up to reality—is the challenge which faces all Wilson's liberal humanists: sometimes it defeats them. Bernard in *Hemlock and After* has won support for a country home for writers, but in his speech at the opening of the house he throws his victory away: 'he seemed quite unable to leave the subject of motivation, so that the more inattentive of his audience got the impression that they were involved in a discussion of some mysterious crime'. What they were involved in was the liberal-humanist death-wish: the failure of will, the fatal self-consciousness, the too-scrupulous conscience which also bedevils Gerald in *Anglo-Saxon Attitudes*.

Wilson's work is valuable as social documentary. He records with great accuracy the changing idiom, habits and fashions of English society in his lifetime: references like the one in 'A Bit Off the Map' to Carroll Levis's Discoveries, a now defunct radio programme, will furnish material for future research students. But the primary aim of his early stories is satirical, not sociological. In story after story he ruthlessly exposes the naked truth, the secret motives and humiliations, behind the public mask of pomposity and self-deception. Many of the early stories contain passages of

violent physical disgust. In 'Union Reunion', set back in
1924 (the year of the Great Empire Exhibition at Wembley,
referred to in the story) South Africa is seen through the
eyes of Laura, a middle–aged woman revisiting her relatives
after many years in England. She is struck by their grossness
and vulgarity: they have been coarsened by years of cheap
food, cheap servants and cheap motor-cars. The cosy
family dinner party is described in language which is deliberately orgiastic:

Stanley himself had seen to the menu and had ordered a massacre in the
poultry-yard that would have challenged Herod—a goose, a turkey,
two ducks and two fowls had all shed their blood that Laura might feel
welcome and Aunt Liz's eighty-eighth birthday not pass unhonoured.

The Biblical allusion turns what is already gross into something cruel and evil. Eating-habits are frequently treated
with disgust, as in the sickening description of Mrs Wrigley's
meal of sardines and stewed tea in her paraffin-heated
cottage (in *Hemlock and After*), or the description, in the
story 'Higher Standards' (included in the third and last
collection of stories, *A Bit Off the Map*, 1957), of a 'grunter',
a baked suet roll filled with unappetising left-overs: 'Mrs
Corfe retained the humour of the tradition by inserting two
burnt currants for the pig's eyes and a sprig of parsley for its
tail.' Wilson frequently uses animal-imagery to give a
disgusted view of humanity. Brian Capper's smile in
'Totentanz' is 'equine with gum-recession'; Gwen in 'Rex
Imperator' 'had retained her peroxide shingle and the rolls
of blue stubbled fat at the back of her neck added to the
bull-dog illusion'.

Wilson is both fascinated and disgusted by characters like
Mrs Wrigley, or Mrs Salad, the Dickensianly-named ex-
lavatory attendant in *Anglo-Saxon Attitudes*. He combines
satire and social documentary in his descriptions of such
characters, who form a kind of sub-world in his early
work. These characters live on the very edge of respecta-
bility, or beyond it. Some are stupid (like Mrs Wrigley);

others, like Ron Wrigley or Mrs Salad's grandson Vin, are on the make, usually by exploiting themselves sexually. A few are wholly evil, notably Mrs Curry in *Hemlock and After*, almost a monstrous Dickensian caricature. Wilson draws a sharp moral distinction between those who exploit themselves and those—like Mrs Curry—who exploit others. It is indeed Ron Wrigley who finally helps to expose Mrs Curry, who conceals her 'business' of procuring a thirteen-year-old girl for a 'respectable' architect under the catchphrase 'We can do with a bit of love in this crazy old world, can't we?' Her definition of 'love' is contrasted in the novel with the romantic guilt-ridden paederasty of the hero, Bernard Sands.

The characters in Wilson's underworld often form parasitical relationships with the respectable. This is particularly true of his homosexual or 'camp' characters (the word occurs in the punning title of one of the chapters of *Hemlock and After*). This world of waiters, designers, interior decorators, theatricals, etc., is almost a sub-culture. Typical Wilson 'camp' characters are Guy in 'Totentanz' with his 'great flair for pastiche' and his 'flat cockney whine', and Sherman in *Hemlock* who also affects this cockney voice. The peculiar brittle, 'bitchy' tone of 'camp' conversation is brilliantly caught in the scene in *Hemlock* in the theatre bar during the interval of Ibsen's *Ghosts* (the choice of this play, with its obsession with family guilt, is significant for the whole novel). Here is Sherman talking to Bernard:

'Terence,' he said, 'is battling at the bar. It suits him to the ground. Pure Barkers' sales. Bless his little Kensington heart. Bernard, my dear, you look tired. Oh, I know, bitching me! Tired equals old. You must make him rest, dear,' he said to Eric; 'you know, feet up and forty winks. Not that I should think you'd be much good at making people rest,' he stared Eric up and down, 'you look a proper little fidget to me.'

Wilson makes these venal and often sad relationships satirically explicit, repudiating the 'gentleman's agreement' by which they used to be regarded as unmentionable or disgusting or embarrassing (compare the reactions of two respectable characters, Gerald in *Anglo-Saxon Attitudes* and Harold in *Late Call*, to the discovery that their sons are homosexual). Christopher Isherwood had described inter-class homosexual relationships through characters like Otto, the beautiful working-class Berlin boy in *Goodbye to Berlin*, but had generally shown them in cosmopolitan settings. Wilson does not show his 'camp' characters as exotics nor are they seen as if by a tourist slumming with a camera. They are shown as part of the very fabric of English society. Ron's attempt to 'pick up' Eric, Sands's boy friend, in *Hemlock and After* takes place in the shadow of St Albans cathedral. Like Dickens, Wilson shows the private links, the secret interdependence, between different worlds.

III

The success of Wilson's early stories lies in their sharp, vivid satirical analyses of people's vulnerability, failure and self-deception. His technique is to show a character as he wishes to appear to others, and as he has succeeded in appearing to himself, and to interpose ironic deflationary comments which reveal the resentments and true motives hidden behind the veneer. Here is the Master of a Scottish university in 'Totentanz': a colleague has just received a legacy and a London Professorship:

'How typical of women,' he said, in the unctuous but incisive voice that convinced so many businessmen and baillies that they were dealing with a scholar whose head was screwed on the right way. 'How typical of women to consider only the legacy. Very nice, of course, a great help in their new sphere.' There was a trace of bitterness, for his own wife's fortune, so important when they started, had vanished through his unfortunate investments. 'But Capper's London Chair is the important thing. A new chair, too, Professor of the History of Technics and Art. Here, of course, we've come to accept so many of Capper's ideas . . .' He paused, staring eagle-like beneath his bushy white eyebrows, the scholar who was judge of men, 'that we forget how revolutionary some of them are', he had indeed the vaguest conception of anything his subordinates thought, an administrator has to keep above detail.

A character frequently satirized in this way is the ex-officer, the gentleman down on his luck, the professional cadger with his sentimental reminiscences of better days. He recurs with minor variations throughout Wilson's work and may be compared with the portrait of the author's father in *The Wild Garden*. He appears as old Mr Nicholson in 'Rex Imperator': he refers to his successful son-in-law, on whom he is sponging, as 'young master Rex', the patronizing tone being a pathetic attempt to cover his resentment and humiliation (Captain Calvert in *Late Call* similarly refers to *his* successful son as 'young master Harold'). When Mr Nicholson 'risked what little cash he still had from Rex's last loan' on a horse, and won, 'like the brave old sportsman he was', the last phrase is the author's satirical comment but is also the character's view of himself ('with all my vices I can safely say I've never been mean').

A more fully realized version of this type is Maurice Legge in the story 'What Do Hippos Eat?' (set, like a later novel, in the London Zoo). Maurice is 'worn out with schemes and lies and phoney deals'. His self-deception is ruthlessly emphasized: 'he had told so many stories for so many years, truth and falsehood were so inextricably mixed, that to check a new falsehood by a poorly remembered old one made him feel that in some way truth must be involved somewhere.' Maurice is in fact no better at facing reality than are privileged idealists like Padley. He thinks he has at last found a girl who will support him, but Greta, for all her 'childlike' manner, and though she admires his old-fashioned style and worldly experience, is not taken in by him: 'Greta's realism had begun at sixteen as a waitress, Maurice's had never really got going: it was hardly an even match.'

The climax of this story, and the point of its title, comes

when Maurice, in order to impress Greta, persuades the keeper of the hippos to take them behind the scenes. But Maurice, who is tired, nearly falls into the pool, and his suit is splashed with mud. The young keeper apologizes but exchanges 'an amused smile' with Greta who says 'It's a terrible old thing anyway. I'm going to get him a new one tomorrow'. Enraged at this snub to his manhood, Maurice puts his hands on Greta and is about to push her into the pool when he is checked by his ignorance of hippos' diet: were they carnivores, 'or would they turn away from the floating Greta in disgust, in which case he would simply have mucked up all his schemes'. So he lets his hands drop, and Greta, who has misinterpreted his gesture as one of affection, puts on her 'wide-eyed' act, turns to him and asks 'What *do* hippos eat, darling?'

Many of the early stories revolve round similar snubs or humiliations. In 'Realpolitik' the pushing newly-appointed administrator-head of an art-gallery snubs his staff; only his admiring secretary remains loyal, but even she punctures his self-esteem and his final thought is 'perhaps a graduate secretary would really be more suitable now'. Other stories which end with a snub are 'Learning's Little Tribute', 'Et Dona Ferentes' and 'Christmas Day in the Workhouse'.

Many of the stories begin on a quiet realistic note and are then pushed deliberately over the edge of realism into a climax of farce, hysteria or violence: the author contrives a situation in which the characters lose control. Thus, after the orgiastic dinner in 'Union Reunion', one of the characters accuses another of letting Laura's young son, many years previously, die through neglect. The most violent climax is the famous ending of 'Raspberry Jam' in which two crazy drunken old women tear a live bird to pieces in front of a child. Violence is blended with farce in the climax of 'A Bit Off the Map' in which a psychotic 'Teddy boy' assaults a mad colonel, and in the macabre party which ends 'Totentanz':

Only the moon lit the vast spaces of Brompton Cemetery, showing up here a tomb and there a yew tree. Professor Cadaver's eyes were wild and his hands shook as he glided down the central pathway. His head still whirled with the fumes of the party and a thousand beautiful corpses danced before his eyes . . . At last he reached his objective—a freshly dug grave on which wooden planks and dying wreaths were piled. The professor began feverishly to tear these away, but he was getting old, and neither his sight nor his steps were as sure as they had been, he caught his foot in a rope and fell nine or ten feet into the tomb. When they found him in the morning his neck was broken. The papers hushed up the affair, and a Sunday newspaper in an article entitled 'Has Science the Right?' only confused the matter by describing him as a professor of anatomy and talking obscurely of Burke and Hare.[1]

Farce and hysteria are extravagantly blended in the tragi-comic scene, in *Hemlock and After*, of the opening of Vardon Hall as a home for writers; the guests get out of control and indulge in 'camp' orgies after a speech by Bernard in which he too loses his 'civilized' self-control and betrays his fears and guilt in a series of 'unfortunate' Freudian slips. In such scenes Wilson offers an almost surrealist distortion of reality.

Wilson uses nuances of speech, not only to 'place' his characters socially and psychologically, but also with satiric intent, to invoke a reaction in the 'knowing' and discriminating reader—usually a kind of wincing distaste. Thus Arthur in 'A Visit in Bad Taste' refers to port as 'very fruity, very tasty' and speaks of 'Nature's call' (Stanley in 'Union Reunion' refers similarly to 'where you can't go for me'.) Maurice Legge calls his heart 'the old ticker' 'even to himself'. Mrs Carrington's verbal mannerisms in 'Mother's Sense of Fun' are mercilessly listed in her son's mind:

He had often thought that to find his mother's phrases one would have to go to English translations of opera or the French and German prose books that he had used at school. It always 'rained cats and dogs', that is if the rain did not 'look like holding off'; Alice Stockfield was 'a bit

---

1 Burke and Hare, notorious body-snatchers in Edinburgh in the eighteen-twenties, provided corpses for surgeons by robbing graves and also by murder.

down in the mouth' but then she 'let things get on top of her'; Roger Grant was 'certainly no Adonis' but she had 'an awfully soft spot in her heart for him'.

Wilson's early stories were first published in *Horizon*, the leading avant-garde literary magazine of the nineteen-forties (it is caricatured as *Survival* by Evelyn Waugh in *Unconditional Surrender*). Yet although the appeal of these early stories is to make the reader feel both clever and fastidious, the style in which they are written shows little regard for elegance, since it consists frequently of breathless, under-punctuated sentences which reflect the sudden release of a long-suppressed creative urge:

Claire was standing by a pot of hydrangeas, the return of physical desire had animated her features as he had not seen them since the early years of their marriage. 'Hullo, Pookie,' he said, 'care for a dance?' The use of her pet name after so many years came strangely to Claire, she knew quite well that his sudden interest was only an interval in the usual routine of their lives, she knew that there was no reciprocal feeling in herself, that she would regret the loss of her new hunger for Tom, but habit was very strong and it shut down upon her emotions, she could not resist an opportunity to strengthen the frayed marital tie.

It is as if, one feels, Claire's thoughts must be recorded quickly, before they can be arranged and (therefore) falsified.

It is as if, too, while offering his first stories to a coterie of the discriminating, Wilson were already probing towards a larger public primarily interested in matter rather than manner, in life rather than art. And in the novels which followed *Anglo-Saxon Attitudes* Wilson seems deliberately to have widened his subject-matter, moving away from both the liberal dilemma and from the 'raffish flotsam' (his own phrase in *The Wild Garden*) of his hotel-childhood, into characters and milieux with which the middle-class novel-reader can identify. And, even in the first two novels, the cleverness and the externalization of the early satirical stories are deepened by the sympathy and understanding with which the central characters are developed.

IV

Wilson's first novel *Hemlock and After* (1952) remains arguably his best because it is the most passionately written. Its theme is Forsterian: the relation between the inner life and the outer, and the whole question of the effectiveness of liberal humanism in our time. Bernard Sands, a successful novelist, is Socratic (hence the book's title) because he ironically and high-mindedly questions accepted values and also because he can be accused of 'corrupting youth'; though married, he has become a practising homosexual. The story moves from victory to disaster—or, looked at in another way, from self-deception to self-knowledge. It starts with Sands triumphant: he has secured Vardon Hall, a local country house, as a home for writers. Because of his personal standing, he has even won government support for his liberal belief that the house should be run without state interference. In a sense, he vouches for an entire moral structure: as soon as he loses confidence in his own motives, his whole world, including Vardon Hall, collapses into chaos. Wilson argues that liberal-humanists tend to fight their battles inside their own consciences rather than against the real evil in the outer world. This evil is portrayed in the book in Mrs Curry the procuress. She too wanted the Hall; Bernard says, 'It would have been interesting to see what she would have made of it'. But this scrupulous and high-minded fairness is at once discredited by the author's comment that Bernard in fact knew very well what she would have made of it—'a second-rate profiteering road-house', or, as a retired admiral more bluntly puts it, 'a high-class knocking-shop'. The dishonesty of liberalism is already apparent.

Sands is forced to face the problem of moral evil not only

through Mrs Curry's activities, of which he learns through his 'camp' connections, but also by his own homosexuality. One night in Leicester Square he sees a man arrested for importuning, and, though he is not himself involved and refuses to give the police any evidence, he realizes that the incident has given him a *frisson*. This incident makes him re-examine the predicament of the individualist in an authoritarian society: 'a humanist, it would seem, was more at home with the wielders of the knout and the rubber truncheon'. A Civil Service friend, Charles Murley, says to Sands, 'You people want the pleasures of authority without any of its penalties.' Sands realizes that the liberal humanist's greatest weakness is that which is also his most precious moral and intellectual luxury: his ambivalence, his freedom to move between two worlds, the world of the Athenaeum and the college high tables, and the world of the Leicester-square bars: the quality that a 'camp' acquaintance refers to less flatteringly as 'versatility'.

By the time of the opening of Vardon Hall Bernard has lost faith in the scheme and in his own authority. Instead of the 'clear, humorous, highminded speech' everyone had expected him to make, he makes a long, confused and 'disastrous' confession of guilt, dwelling on evil and defeat. Afterwards he says 'I see Nothing behind nothing', echoing the anti-vision of the Marabar caves in Forster's *A Passage to India*. He has now made his choice and has puzzled both his respectable and his 'camp' friends. 'I must stand with the unfortunate', he writes in his last letter, just before he dies.

Because of what Murley refers to as 'his mood of exaggerated conscience' Bernard cannot bring himself to denounce Mrs Curry publicly. This is done by his wife Ella after his death. During his earlier period of triumph Ella had been in a state of neurotic withdrawal from the world, and this is structurally related to Bernard's withdrawal into sickness and despair in the second half of the book. When he dies, Ella comes back to life. At the end of the book their daughter says to Ella: 'It seems strange that his books will have such influence when in his life he got so little done. I suppose it's because you were always the doer.' 'My dear,' Ella replies, 'doing doesn't last, even if one knows what one's doing, which one usually doesn't'.

The point that 'doing doesn't last' is neatly illustrated when we learn that Mrs Curry used her time in prison, from which she was released after two years as a result of good behaviour, to form 'a most useful group of loving dutiful girls through whom she could bring snugness and cosiness to respectable gentlemen'. Bernard's failure in the world of action is further illustrated by another irony: after his death, Vardon Hall is to be run by a public relations man, 'quite young and very pushing', clearly a similar type to the administrators in 'Realpolitik' and *The Mulberry Bush*. Bernard deliberately destroyed his own 'charisma'; yet he died content, retaining a kind of innocence. Ella sees him as a small boy. Like many of Wilson's characters, he never grows up. Even the self-knowledge he attains is masochistic. Murley's loyalty to him seems exaggeratedly deferential, though this is perhaps necessary to balance the dislike of Mrs Curry and of Eric's mother. Wilson's whole treatment of him is more romantic than anything in the later novels.

The humanist crisis of conscience is more objectively examined in the next novel, *Anglo-Saxon Attitudes* (1956), the best plotted of all Wilson's novels. The title, taken from *Alice*, exemplifies the author's addiction at this time to jokes, puns and clichés in his titles and chapter-headings: it refers not only to the Anglo-Saxon period (the novel is about medieval historians) but also to that elusive complex of attitudes and prejudices which make up the English temperament during the present time, in which the action of the book is set.

In 1912, before the action proper begins, a pagan idol was discovered in the tomb of a seventh-century bishop excavated at Melpham in East Anglia by the late Professor Stokesay, a medievalist who in his last years discredited his profession by becoming a political journalist and pro-Nazi. (The 'find' is elaborately documented by Wilson in a 'spoof' appendix.) The discovery has led some medievalists to construct theories about the survival of paganism in early Christian England. The plot turns on the probability that the idol was planted in the tomb by Stokesay's son Gilbert, a neurotic poet killed in the first world war. Such a joke, perpetrated out of revenge against a too-famous father and a youthful iconoclast's desire to show up the vanity and lack of imagination of scholars, might be hard to explain outside England (the England that produced Butler's *The Way of All Flesh* and Gosse's *Father and Son*), and this is part of the point of the novel. It may seem a rather technical theme for a long book, but the result is a fascinating detective story as well as an exploration of the character of English intellectuals during the forty years between the first world war and the nineteen-fifties.

The forty years are the adult life of Gerald Middleton, the novel's hero, a retired professor of medieval history. In a long reverie which forms most of the first half of the novel he re-lives many of the earlier events of his life. Despite —or because of—his charm and distinction he feels he has failed both in his personal and in his professional career. He has failed as a husband (he lives apart from his wife) as a father (his children ignore him) and as a lover (his ex-mistress, Dollie, Gilbert Stokesay's widow, has become a dipsomaniac). He also doubts the value of historical studies. His failure to face up to the truth is symbolized by his failure to voice his suspicions (based on a clearly-remembered conversation with Gilbert when the latter was drunk) that the Melpham idol was a hoax. Thus the central theme of the novel continues the inner debate begun in *Hemlock and After;* but while Bernard dies, Gerald at last succeeds in confessing his suspicions about Melpham and resumes his long-neglected historical work.

Like Sands, Gerald has an 'exaggerated conscience'.

His friend and mentor, Sir Edgar Iffley, *doyen* of English medievalists, finds Gerald's handling of the Melpham affair 'finicking and high-strung', 'typical of these rich tradespeople' (the Middletons run a family business from which Gerald, though taking no part, draws large dividends), 'more like a Dissenter than a gentleman'. Once again, Wilson is analysing the nonconformist conscience as seen in a certain type of cultivated English intellectual.

At the very end of the book, Sir Edgar is seeing Gerald off at London airport on a trip to Mexico. They run into Clarissa Crane, a second-rate novelist whom we met in the opening chapter, when she attended a meeting of medievalists (this meeting is perhaps the most brilliantly observed scene in all Wilson's writing) in search of copy. Sir Edgar had then taken a dislike to Miss Crane, putting her down as a time-waster. Now she criticizes Middleton to him for not having done much with his life (the same criticism as that made of Sands at the end of the previous novel). Sir Edgar answers 'I can imagine someone who hardly knew him at all thinking so', and departs, thinking (and these are the last words of the book) 'God knows who the woman was— never seen her face or heard her name before. One thing was perfectly clear to him, however: she was a time-waster'.

Once again, Wilson's own sympathies towards an ambivalent central character are clear. It is significant that Gilbert, who perpetrated the Melpham fraud, was a disciple of Hulme and Wyndham Lewis, who opposed the Bloomsbury liberal tradition. Wilson maintains that this tradition, for all its vulnerability and self-doubt, remains more attractive and also more valuable than anything else in English intellectual and moral life. In satirical contrast to Middleton stands Professor Clun, unattractive, efficient in research, a man who could never suffer a psychological *bloc* or a crisis of conscience. The judgment that it is better to fail with Middleton than succeed with Clun is characteristic of 'Bloomsbury'.

Besides its main theme, *Anglo-Saxon Attitudes* (the most

spacious and Dickensian of Wilson's novels) contains
several sub-plots, built around members of Middleton's
family, his fellow-historians (there are a number of delight-
ful satirical portraits for those who know this world) and
the survivors of Melpham; some of these sub-plots also
take us into the 'camp' world.

Meg, the heroine of Wilson's next novel, *The Middle Age
of Mrs Eliot* (1958) is a female version of Gerald Middleton.
She too is rich, charming, attractive, sensual, a dilettante by
temperament (both collect works of art): she even 'drawls'
like Middleton. Her husband Bill—a successful though
rather neurotic barrister—dies suddenly early in the book,
in Forsterian style, and the novel is the story of how Meg
re-builds her life. The book is, however, less interesting, I
think, than its two predecessors. Meg tends to collapse into a
set of rather tiresome mannerisms (such as her habit of
saying 'Dear God'). Meg's perceptions are treated more
schematically, more externally, than Bernard's or Gerald's.
One is perhaps reminded of E. M. Forster's treatment of
Helen Schlegel in *Howards End*. Yet Wilson has said in
The Wild Garden that he consciously identified himself
with Meg rather than with her two predecessors, and that he
sought to relate her dilemma—a crisis of despair followed by
a new self-knowledge—to his own. We are told in the novel
that Meg was 'made to judge', which puts her with Bernard
and Gerald: like them, too, she looks ironically on her own
conclusions yet is also (in a curious way typical of the liberal
sensibility) satisfied with them: so that her final self-assess-
ment—'I'm quite a silly person really'—does not emerge as a
criticism. Wilson has tried to disengage himself from a
personal dilemma by transposing it into a partly alien world.
The transposition is perhaps not entirely convincing. Meg
seems to be sometimes 'at home', sometimes a fish out of
water.

The book's other main character is Meg's brother, David,
who has abandoned the academic world to keep a market
garden in Sussex with Gordon, a homosexual friend. In

The Wild Garden Wilson stresses the importance of garden-
ing in his work and in his life since he left the Museum and
made his home in a cottage in East Anglia. But I do not think
he makes this subject interesting. Perhaps it is something
one has to do, not write about. David's house, with its
Saxon name (Andredaswood), is perhaps a symbol of English
life in retreat: indeed, the novel has echoes, both in this
symbolic house, and in the heroine's name, of *Howards End*.
But David's life seems sterile, like his relationship with
Gordon. After Gordon's death David toys with the idea of
going back to research. Just before Meg leaves Andredaswood, where she has been recuperating, there is a brief
nursery idyll in which she helps her brother to rearrange his
notes on eighteenth-century fiction. But David's eremitical
detachment is alien to Meg's worldly energy. Having used
each other, they go their separate ways.

Meg's rehabilitation is depicted rather on the level of an
article on a superior 'woman's page': as a lesson in 'pluck',
in 'managing'—the kind of attitude the earlier Wilson might
have satirized. Perhaps because one is antagonized by Meg's
'enviable' coolness and 'exotic' glitter at the beginning of the
book, one feels little sympathy for her later vulnerability.
Meg has virtues, notably adaptability, courage and independence, and for these one may admire her; but she
remains somehow hard to like, while the other characters
never really come to life.

The Old Men at the Zoo (1961) is an ambitious attempt to
break new ground. Set in the nineteen-seventies, it is about
who shall run England; a moral fable on the theme that
power corrupts. The London Zoo is not only, in the novel,
the famous national institution; it also becomes, like England
itself, a battleground of conflicting values and interests; its
various administrators are the traditional bureaucracy, whose
failure is shown as both disastrous and degrading. After a
brief and rather unconvincing war, England emerges
committed to 'Pan-Europeanism', which is revealed as even
more unsavoury than the *ancien régime*. When the Zoo

reopens, its new Director, a central European scholar ironically named Englander, allows it to be used for unscholarly and disgusting propaganda. Thus 'an old mangy Siberian bear' is exhibited with one leg tethered and the label 'The Russian Bear in difficulties'. Later, one of the 'new men'—the kind of men, it is suggested, whom violence brings to power—wants to stage public fights in the Zoo between animals and political prisoners. Englander is sent to prison for acquiescing in this suggestion and the last of the 'old men' has gone. At the end of the book there is a characteristically Wilsonian episode in which Simon Carter, the book's narrator, Secretary of the Zoo and now a candidate for the Directorship, faces the Vice-President, Professor Hales, an unsympathetic figure, rather like Clun in *Anglo-Saxon Attitudes*. Hales refers to the past as a 'very bad period' (and as with Clun, the *judgment* is correct—it is the *tone*, the lack of insight, which are criticized). He asks Carter how he feels about 'the new world before us'. Carter's answer is that of the unrepentant humanist: 'It excites me enormously, especially because I shall always be involved with the old'.

Carter is torn—in a typically Wilsonian dilemma—between administration and scholarship. When he has to act in a crisis, he says, 'I needed all my irony to protect myself from the absurd pretension of the action', and this need for irony is characteristic. The question is, can a man keep his integrity in a world of power? As in *Hemlock and After*, personal vulnerability affects public decisions. Earlier in the book, a plan to start a nature reserve in the country is defeated by the forces of reaction (who want to keep the Zoo as a popular London spectacle) and by a scandal involving the nymphomaniac daughter of the then Director.

The Zoo animals are shown as the victims of human violence and stupidity. At the beginning of the book a giraffe, most harmless of large animals, accidently kills a keeper; then an Alsatian dog is shot because of human

concupiscence; in the war, Carter kills and eats a badger—
another large harmless animal on which he is an amateur
authority.

For all its detail and its intelligence, and despite some
very powerful scenes especially in the second half, this
novel does not, I think, succeed in holding the reader's
unflagging attention throughout its great length in the way
Anglo-Saxon Attitudes did. This may be partly due to the use
of first-person narration. It is not a technique which suits
this author: the other example of it, the first half of the
story 'A Bit Off the Map', is also unsuccessful (the second
half, when the device is abandoned, is far better). We are
obliged to take Carter at his rather dull face-value, and he
tends to blur and confuse some of the events.

With *Late Call* (1964) Wilson returns to the high comedy
of his earlier manner: yet also offers, in Sylvia Calvert, one
of his most sympathetic central figures. This is perhaps
the most enjoyable of the later novels. After a poor country
childhood (described in a curious and touching prologue
which is almost a Lawrentian short-story) Sylvia marries:
but her husband, Arthur, 'the Captain', has never got over
the first world war and has ever since led a disreputable yet
somehow defiant saloon-bar existence. Sylvia has therefore
had to work all her life, as a hotel manageress. When the
novel proper opens, the couple are coming to live with their
son Harold in Carshall New Town. Harold, a widower,
with teen-age children, is a successful schoolmaster, with an
extrovert, hearty, patronizing manner and a tiresome sense
of humour which prevents self-criticism. His 'new-style'
progressivism is well-intentioned but spiritually blinkered.
He lacks the saving Wilsonian irony and is consequently
fair game for ironic treatment. The family set-up is splen-
didly satirized. When Sylvia, unused to central heating,
dares to adjust the thermostat Harold, highly offended,
issues a 'rota' of household duties which ends 'Temperature
Control: Harold'. He has a boyish enthusiasm for his
'ranch-type' house and for the expensive gadgets which his

extra income from writing text-books has brought him. His demonstration to his mother of his electric cooker— with its 'autotimer' fitted with a specially muted 'pinger'— is brilliantly held on the very edge of caricature:

'Now take this meal we're cooking this evening. Of course it's not a normal meal. I've specially designed it to illustrate all the equipment,' he smoothed his moustache with a certain pride. 'The goulash in your top oven. And just for this evening—an example of conspicuous waste— an apfelstrudel in your lower oven. Of course, that's really reserved for the big fellows, turkeys and such, and for any fiestas. We'll bake there for this little party we're giving for you before Christmas. Then, on the drop-in hob—soup for Dad on the simmerstat, and on the two hob-points two veg, also for my conservative-minded parents'—he winked at her—'and then a special treat for Dad, whose true blue palate can't take goulash—a half chicken for the grill. Frankly I shouldn't have pandered to him like this if it hadn't been a very useful way of demonstrating the roto-roaster.'

Like Meg Eliot, like nearly all Wilson's heroes and heroines, Sylvia has to come to terms with a new life. And this involves, as so often, a judgment between two ways. Despite Harold's patronage Sylvia manages to assert her independence. She refuses to be put out to grass in the humanely heartless modern way. Her furniture is shabby and doesn't fit in, but though itself valueless it somehow manages to question the value of Harold's status-symbols. And her natural East Anglian good sense and dignity—even though somewhat overlaid by simple clichés from low-brow fiction and television—contain more wisdom than the committees and communal schemes over which Harold wears himself out.

At the end of the book there is a family crisis in which Harold discovers that one of his sons is homosexual. He reacts, not like Gerald (who faced the same problem with detachment in *Anglo-Saxon Attitudes*) but with conventional anger, and throws himself with fresh gusto into work. His mother decides to set up on her own (Arthur has now died).

She has made an independent friendship with an American family through whom she re-lives a little of her own past. She realizes that her son does not need her: they operate in different worlds. If we care more about her than we do about Meg Eliot, this is perhaps both because she is a nicer person and because she has been provided with a more interesting fictional context.

No Laughing Matter (1967) is Wilson's longest and most complex novel to date. An undoubted tour-de-force, it has no proper plot, but is a series of episodes or 'takes' which follow the fortunes of the Matthews family through the changing social and political fashions of the last half-century (like *Anglo-Saxon Attitudes*, it goes back to 1912—there are other resemblances also, though the Matthewses are more theatrical and highly-coloured than the Middletons). The narrative is interspersed with playlets which parody various contemporary dramatic styles, and in which members of the family play all the parts, as in charades. In some of the sketches, the identities of the various members of the family merge into one another: Wilson here uses a technique rather like that of Joyce in the 'Night-town' fantasy in *Ulysses*.

The father, 'Billy Pop', who has the same Christian name as the author's own father, is a familiar Wilson 'type': a self-pitying failed writer. The mother, 'the Countess', has vitality and lovers. The cockney servant, Regan, is like Mrs Salad in *Anglo-Saxon Attitudes*. Most of the children become successful—Rupert as an actor, Quentin as a womanizing political journalist and, in his later years, a television pundit (like John Middleton), Marcus as a homosexual art-dealer, Margaret as a novelist. With Margaret Wilson seems to identify more closely than with any of his previous characters: her literary career is a paradigm of his own, and through her self-criticisms he explores some of his own problems as a creative writer. Her early stories are 'wonderfully nasty': 'you catch them without their bathing-trunks, don't you?' says someone.

Her first subject is her own family (disguised as the Car-
michaels) and at one point a parallel is suggested with
Margaret Kennedy's famous best-seller about a bohemian
family, *The Constant Nymph*. Margaret repudiates the
parallel, but it is clearly intended to enter the reader's mind
as a possible 'treatment'.

This question of treatment is important in the book,
which explores technical problems about the relation
between 'art' and 'reality', between texture and theme:
a kind of experimental documentary. Wilson seems to be
reassessing the 'panorama' of English family life as a literary
mode. Can the 'saga' still come off? Must it involve parody?
Can it be 'aesthetic' as well as 'social'? A character makes this
point about Galsworthy—again, Margaret dismisses him,
but that is in 1937: today, he is enormously popular, and
the television version of *The Forsyte Saga* is mentioned in the
last chapter of the novel. Thus, *No Laughing Matter* offers
in its very title an ambivalent attitude to its subject. The
questions it raises are important to Wilson, who has here
tried to reflect an even larger area of English life than in his
previous books. The fact that English families have so often
been treated cosily and sentimentally (as in radio and
television sagas, or in Noel Coward's famous period-piece
Cavalcade) is also relevant. 'The family' so often has a Peter
Pan quality. The Matthewses grow older in each 'take',
yet somehow never grow up: and the author's awareness
of this is part of the irony.

I cannot analyse here all the implications of this long and
often very funny novel, which will probably only be seen
in perspective when we can relate it to its successors as well
as to its author's earlier 'family' stories. But it indicates
again Wilson's vitality and intellectual range. His creative
career has now lasted twenty years, during which time he has
published much literary journalism and criticism (including
a series of lectures on 'Evil in the English novel'), besides
his fiction. As a novelist he has concentrated on English
character and behaviour, but has also tried to relate these

afresh in each novel to the changing character of English society. His irony has grown warmer, and now seems a kind of protective envelope, a necessary self-indulgence which is both our weakness as a nation and our strength.

ANGUS WILSON

A Select Bibliography

(Place of publication London, unless stated otherwise)

Separate Works:

THE WRONG SET (1949). *Stories*
SUCH DARLING DODOS (1950). *Stories*
EMILE ZOLA (1952). *Critical Study*
HEMLOCK AND AFTER (1952). *Novel*
FOR WHOM THE CLOCHE TOLLS: A SCRAPBOOK OF THE TWENTIES (with P. Jullian) (1953).
THE MULBERRY BUSH (1956). *Play*
ANGLO-SAXON ATTITUDES (1956). *Novel*
A BIT OFF THE MAP (1957). *Stories*
THE MIDDLE AGE OF MRS ELIOT (1958). *Novel*
THE OLD MEN AT THE ZOO (1961). *Novel*
THE WILD GARDEN, or speaking of writing (1963)
—a series of lectures given in California in 1960.
LATE CALL (1964). *Novel*
NO LAUGHING MATTER (1967). *Novel*
'Evil in the English Novel', *The Listener*, 27 Dec. 1962, 3, 10, 17 Jan. 1963
—based on the Northcliffe Lectures, 1961.
WRITERS AT WORK, ed. M. Cowley (1958)
—contains interview of A. Wilson by M. Millgate.

Some Biographical and Critical Studies

'Favoured Sons: The Moral World of Angus Wilson', by A. O. J. Cockshut, *Essays in Criticism*, Vol. IX, 1, 1959.
'Angus Wilson', by I. Scott-Kilvert, *A Review of English Literature*, Vol. I, 2, 1960.
POST-WAR BRITISH FICTION, by J. Gindin; University of California, Los Angeles (1962).
THE FREE SPIRIT, by C. B. Cox (1963).
ANGUS WILSON, by J. L. Halio (1964)
—Writers and Critics series. Contains a bibliography of Wilson's literary journalism.
THE REACTION AGAINST EXPERIMENT IN THE ENGLISH NOVEL, 1950–1960, by R. Rabinovitz; Columbia University Press (1967).
THE SITUATION OF THE NOVEL, by B. Bergonzi (1969).